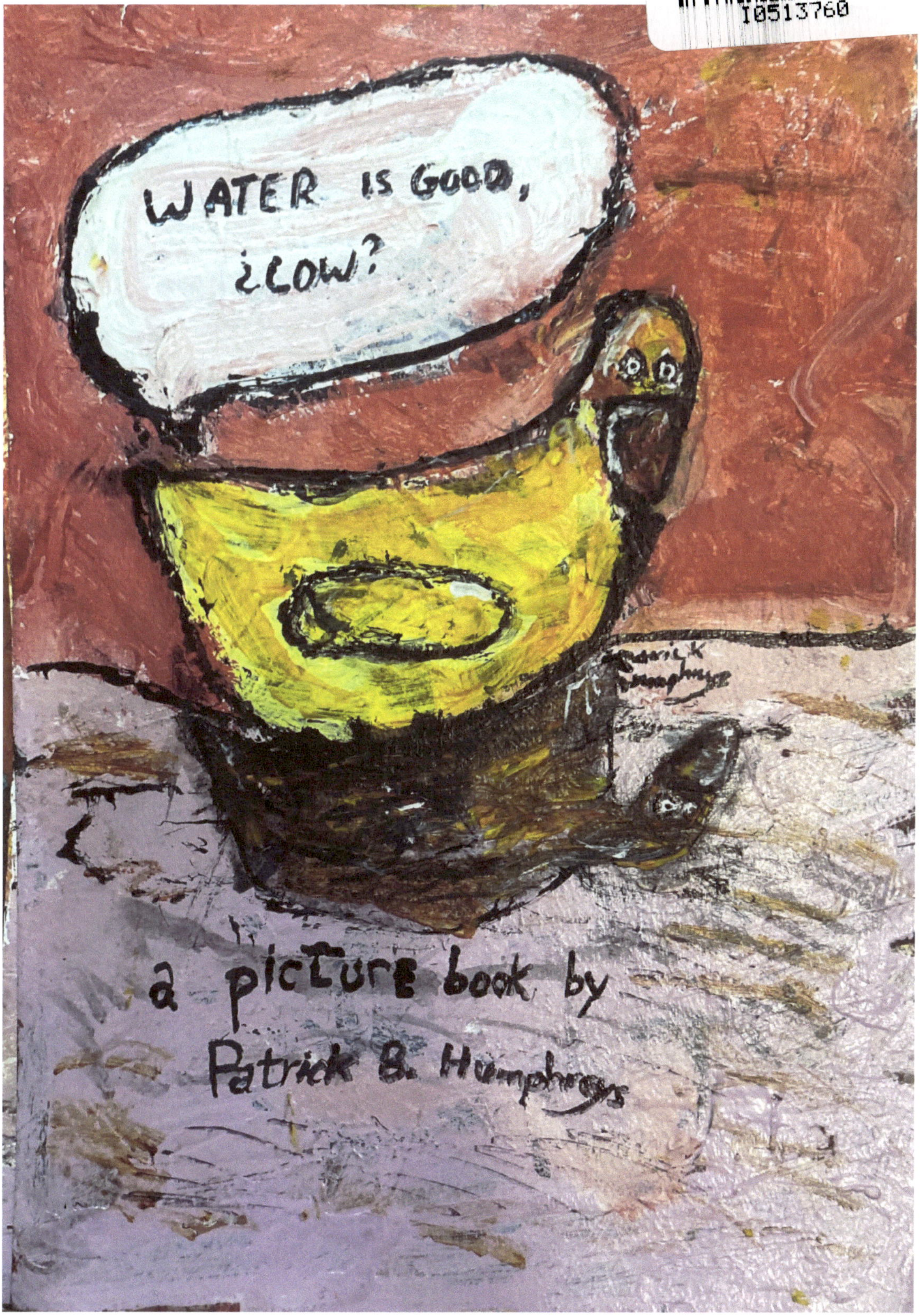
WATER IS GOOD,
¿COW?
a picture book by
Patrick B. Humphreys

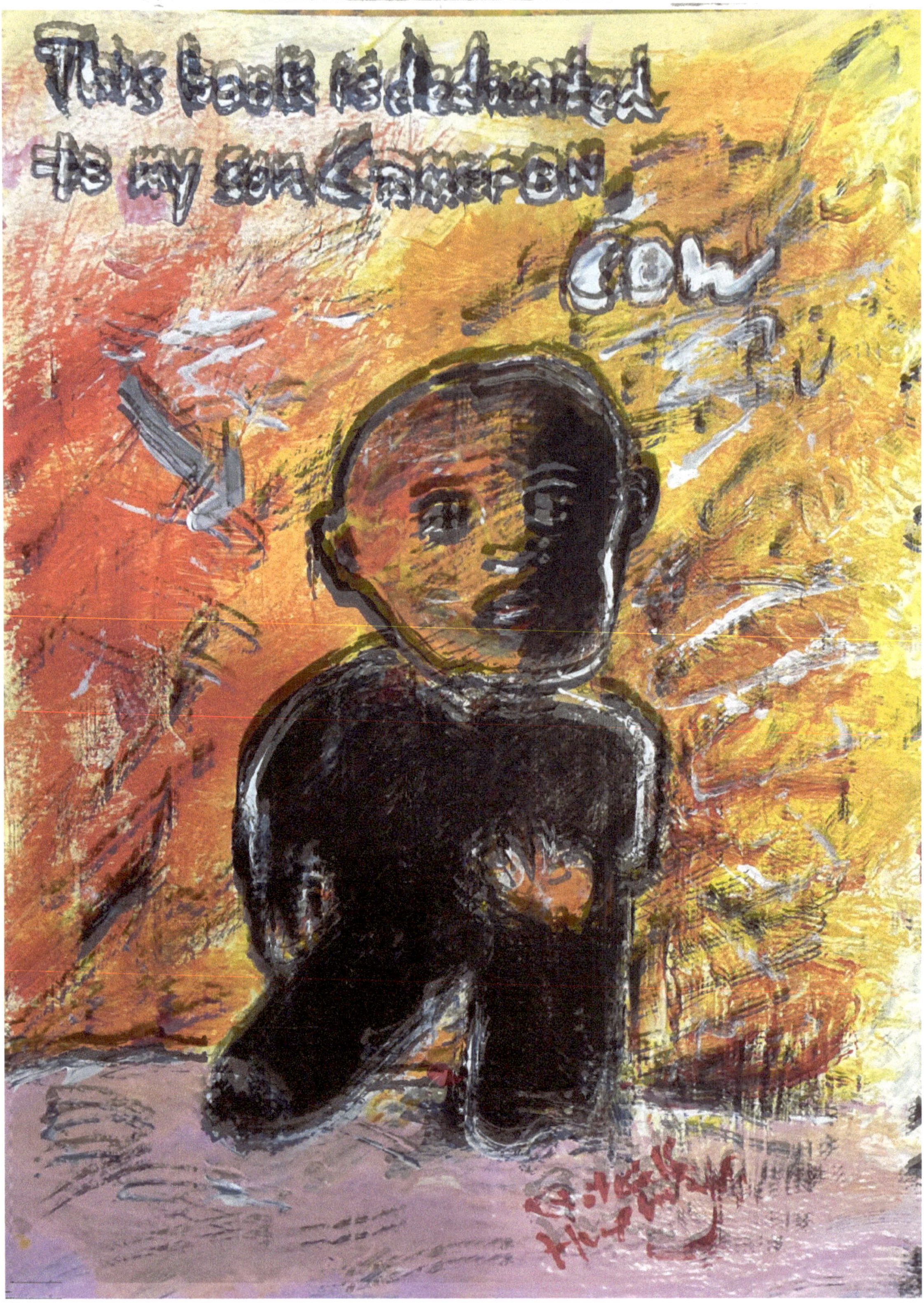
This book is dedicated to my son Cameron
COW

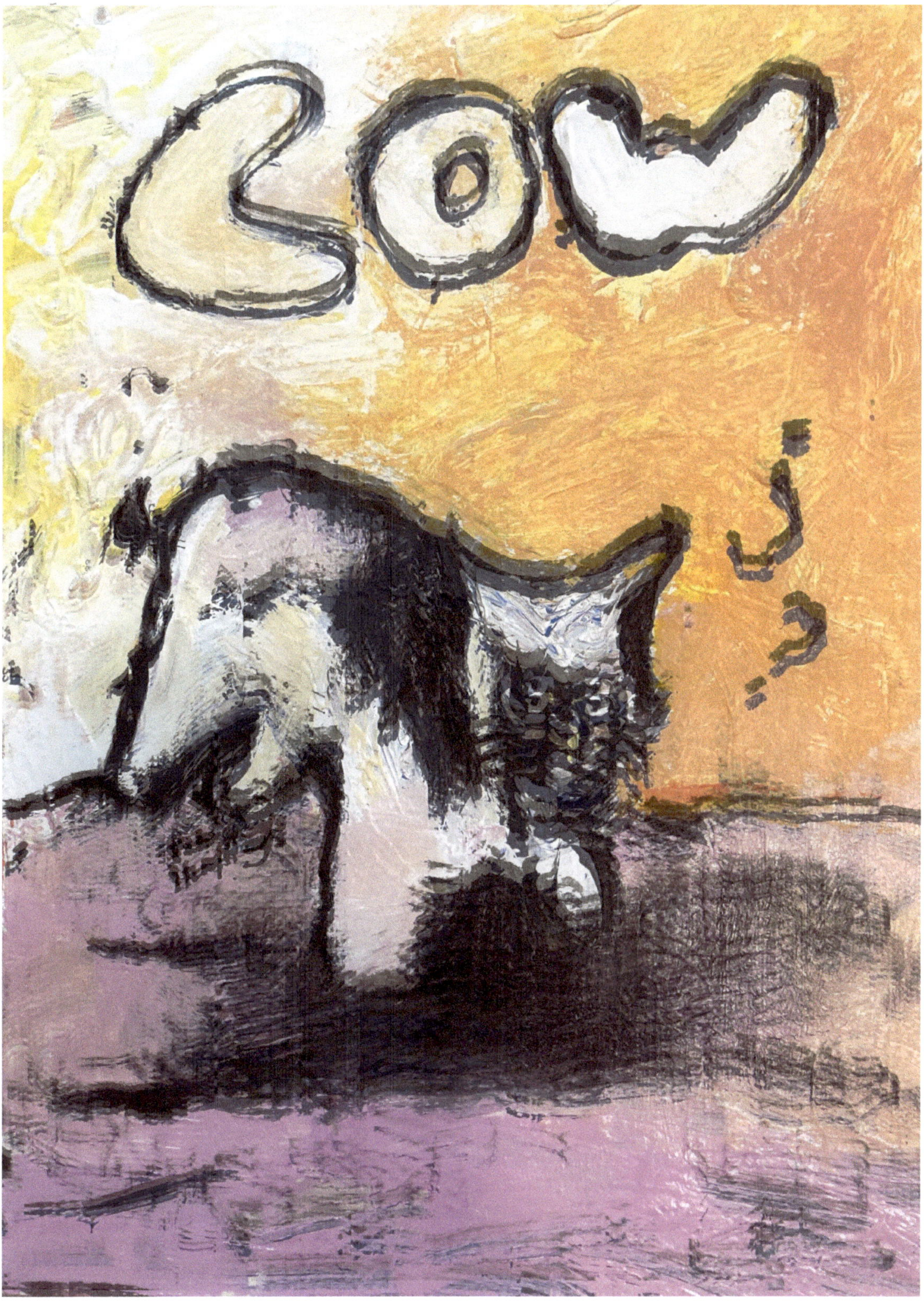
Cow

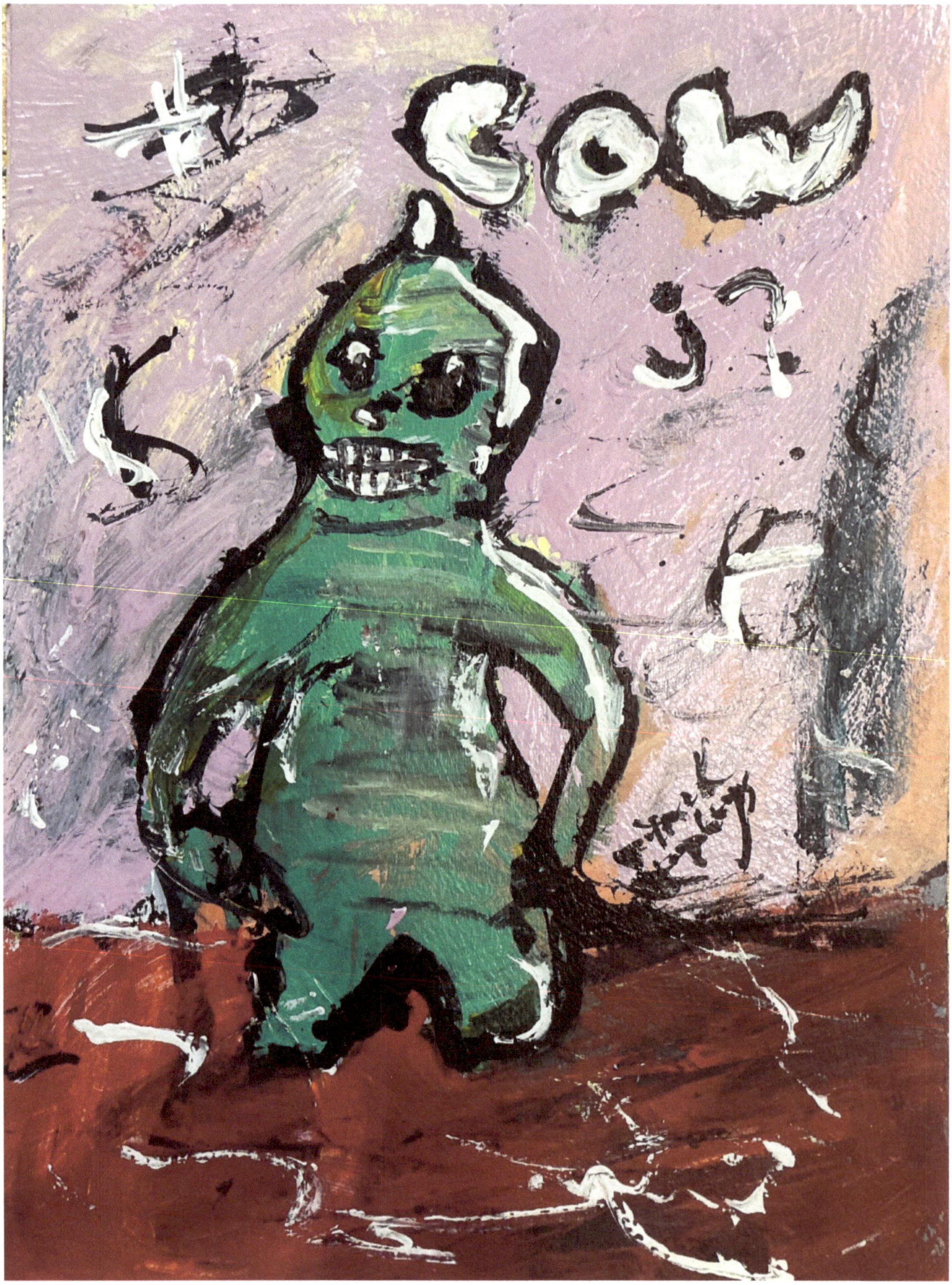
COW

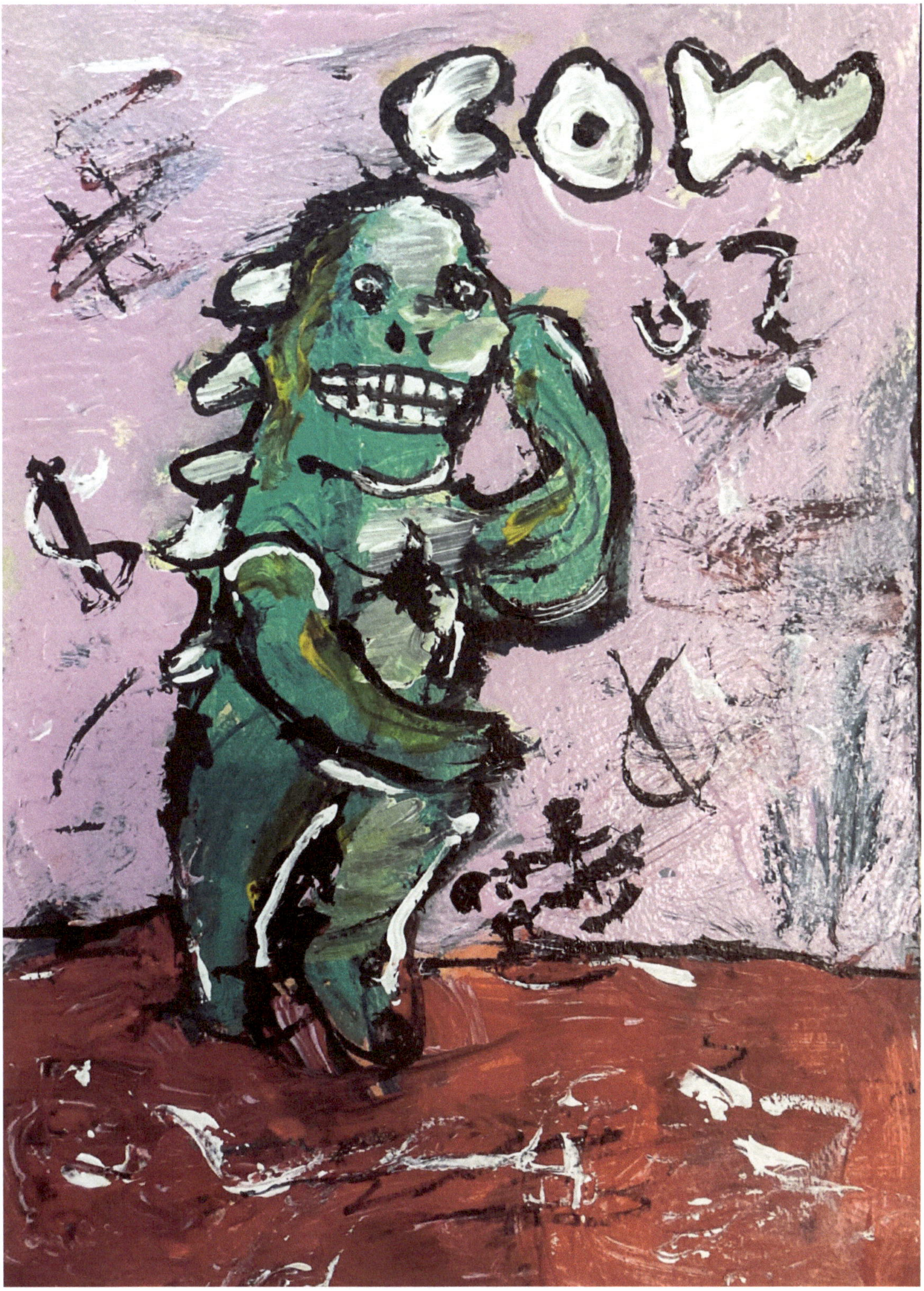
COW

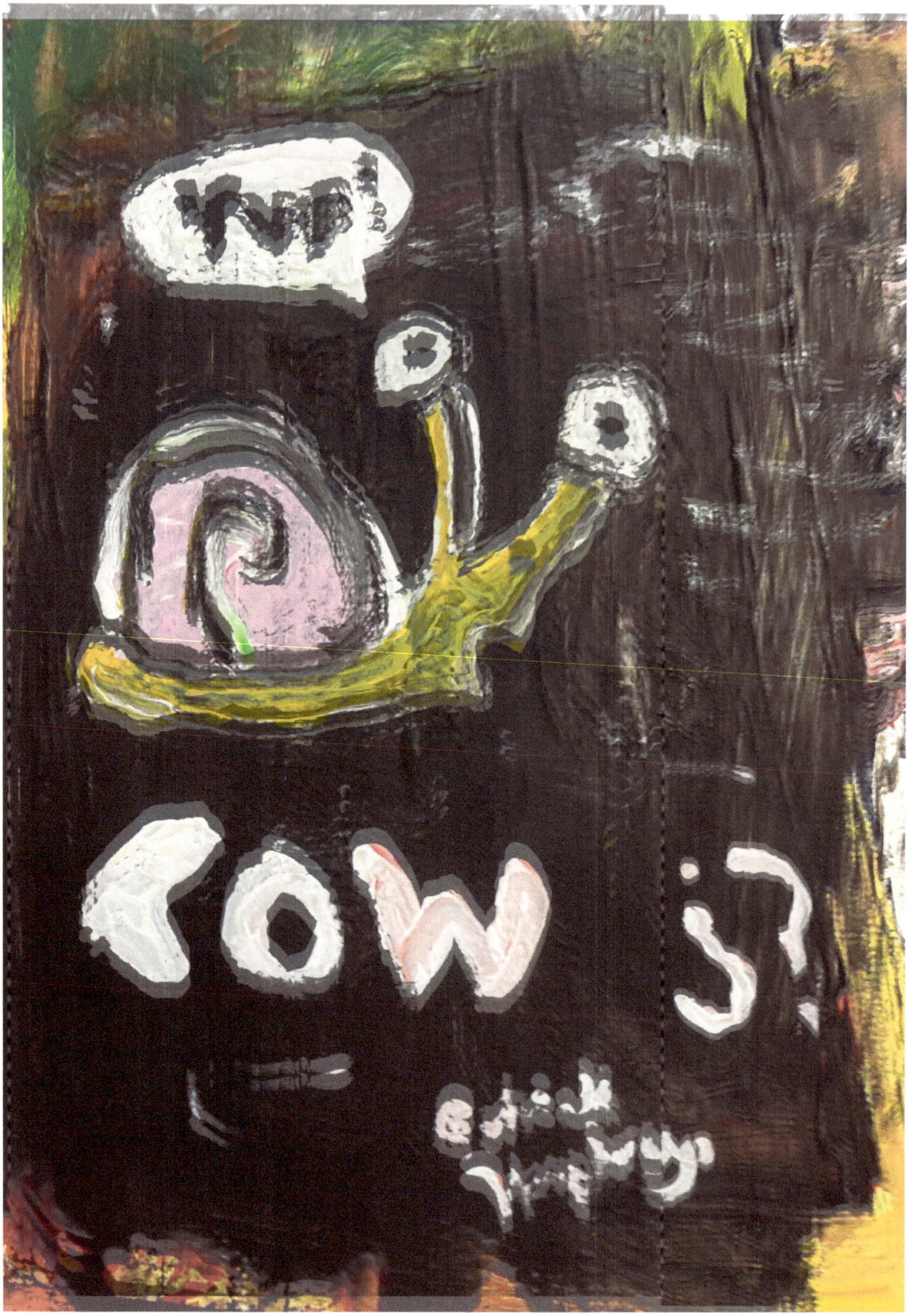
cow ¿?

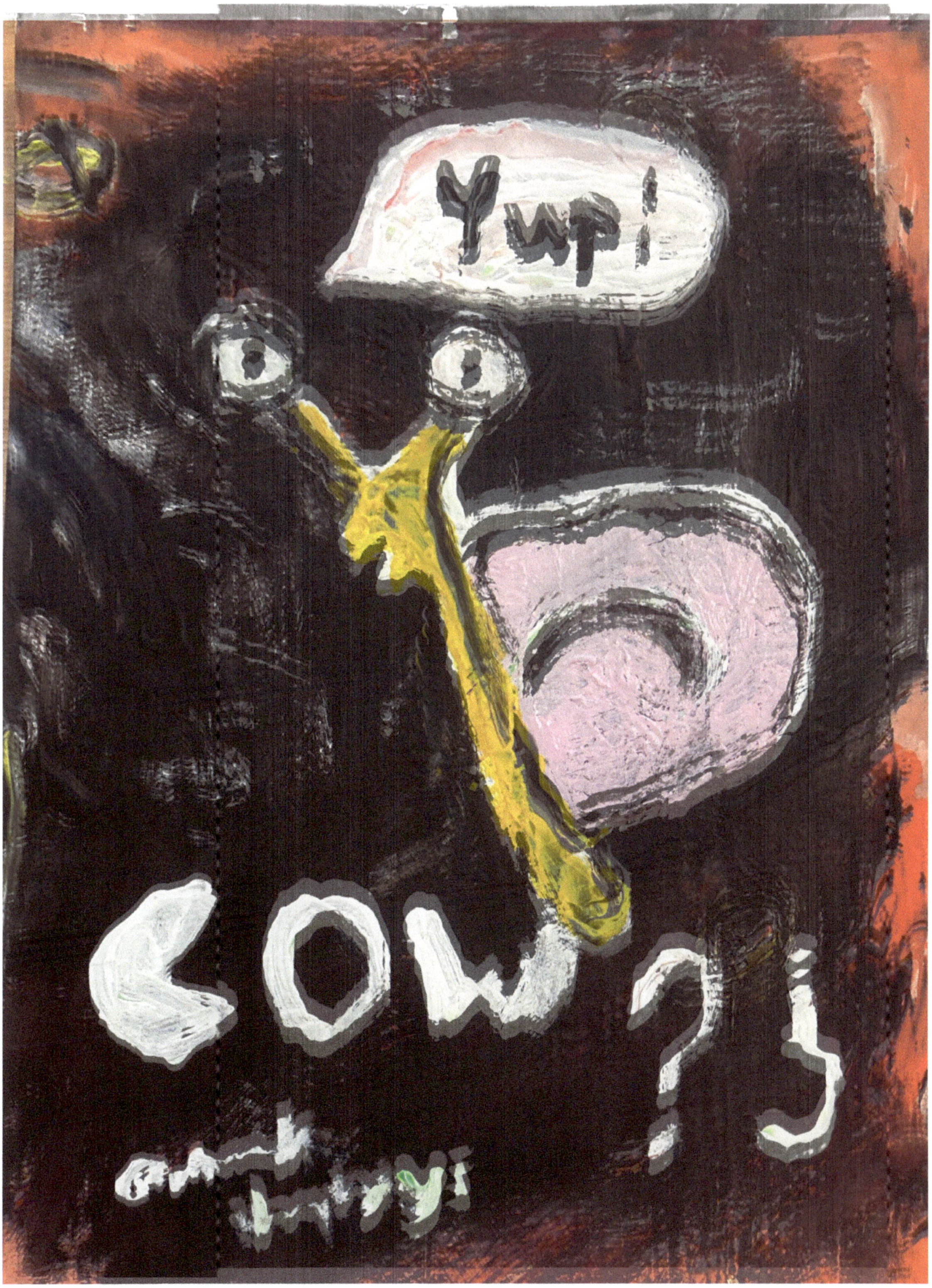
Yup!
cow?¿

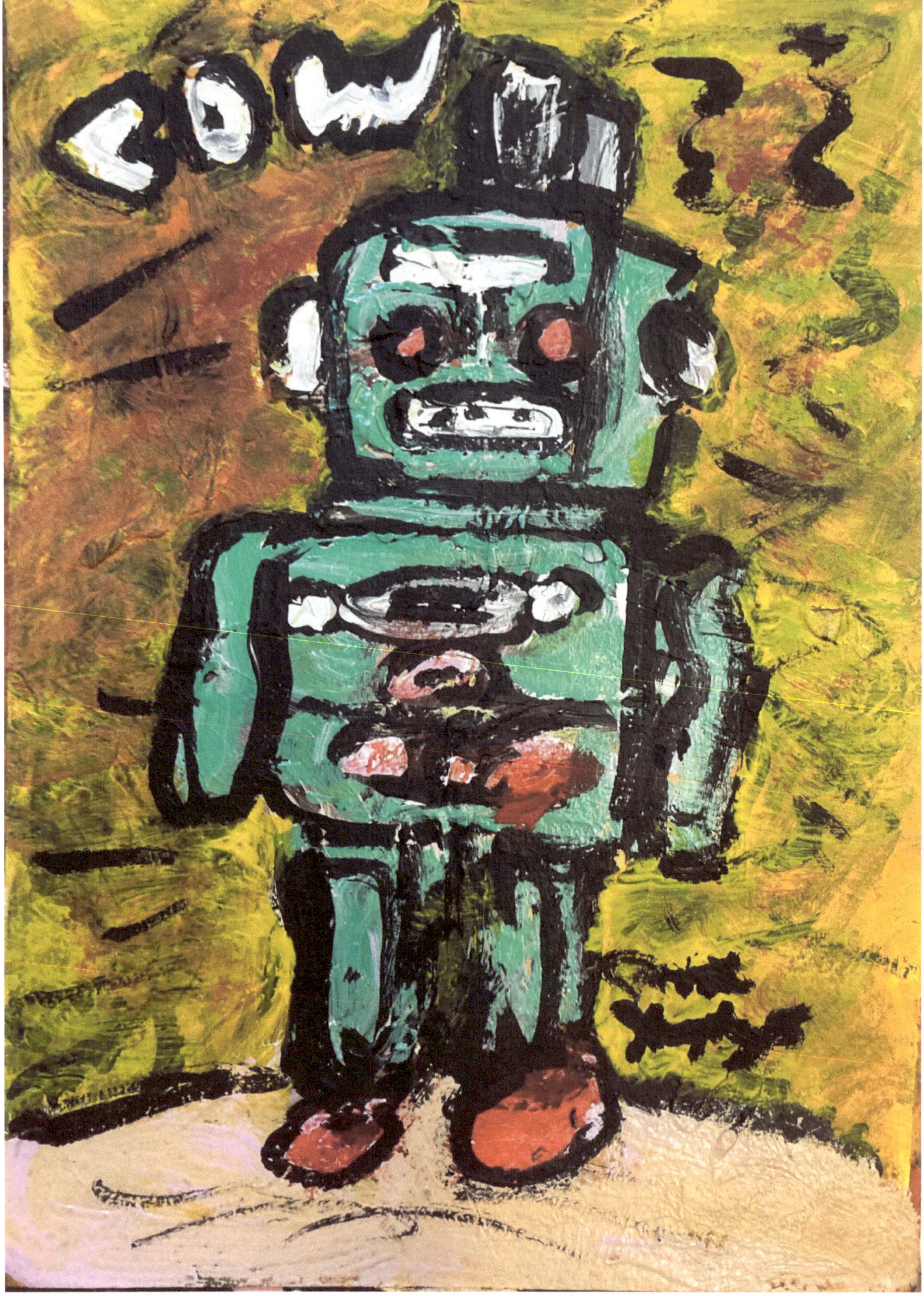

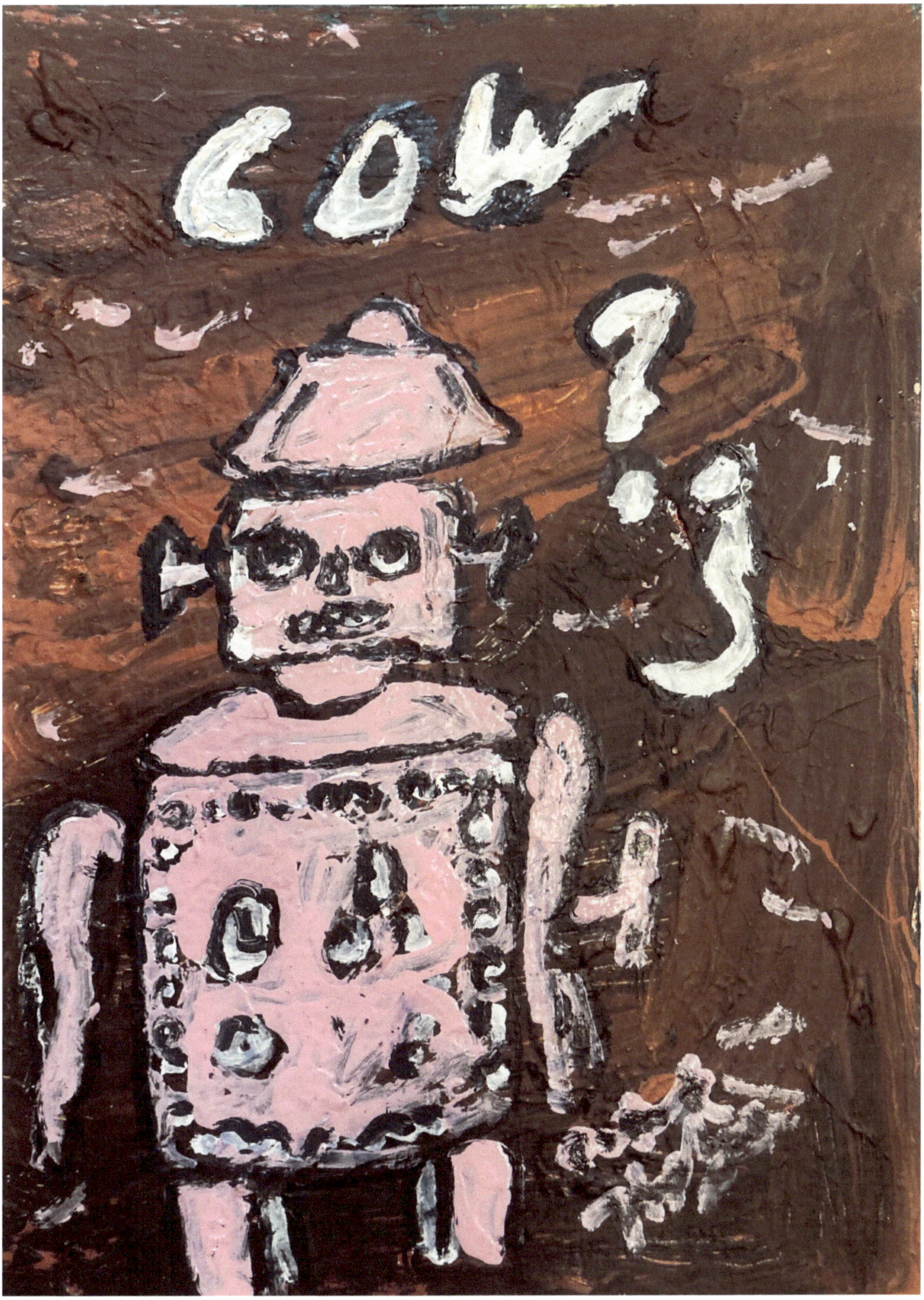
COW
?

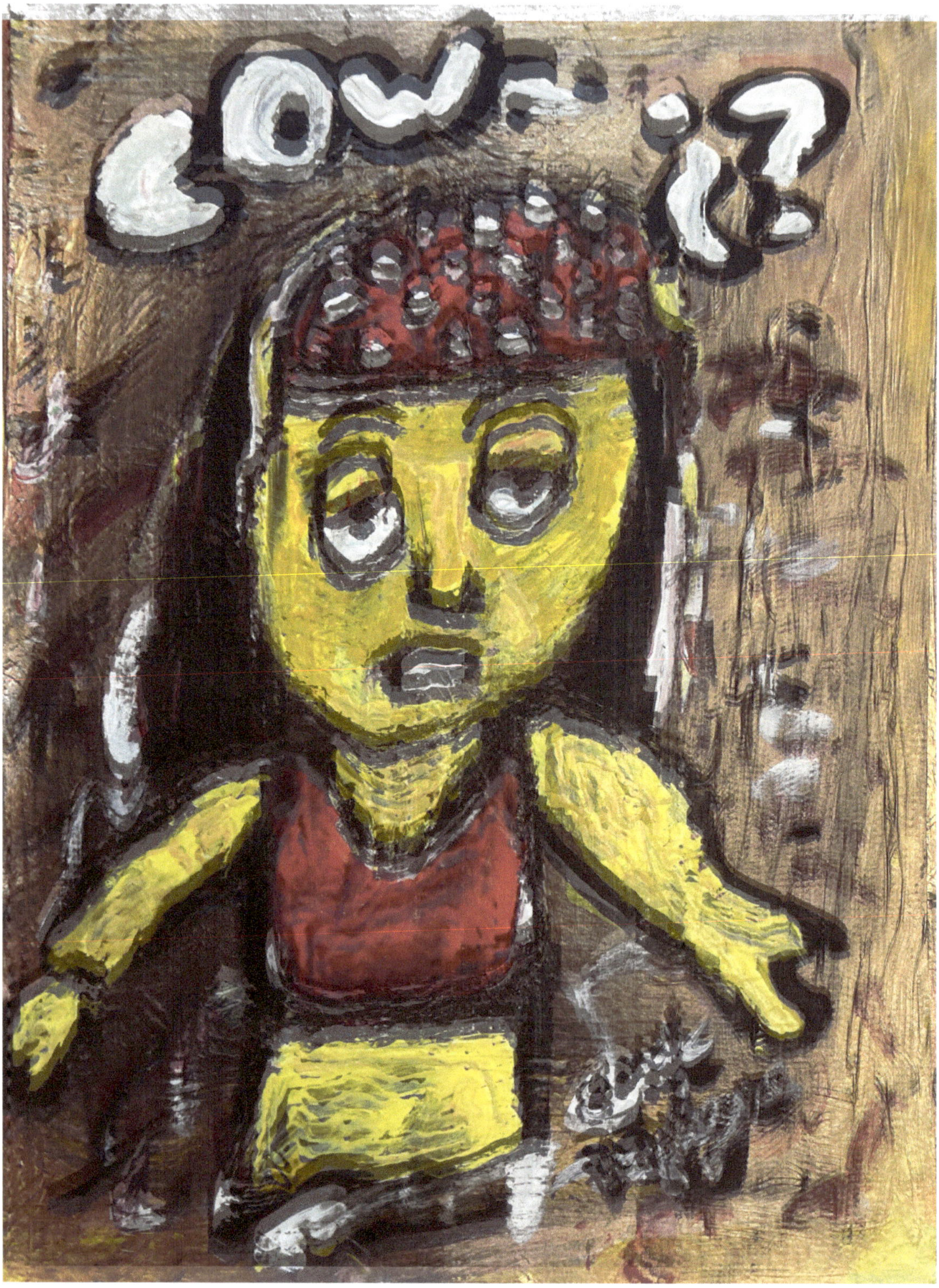
COW-. ¿?

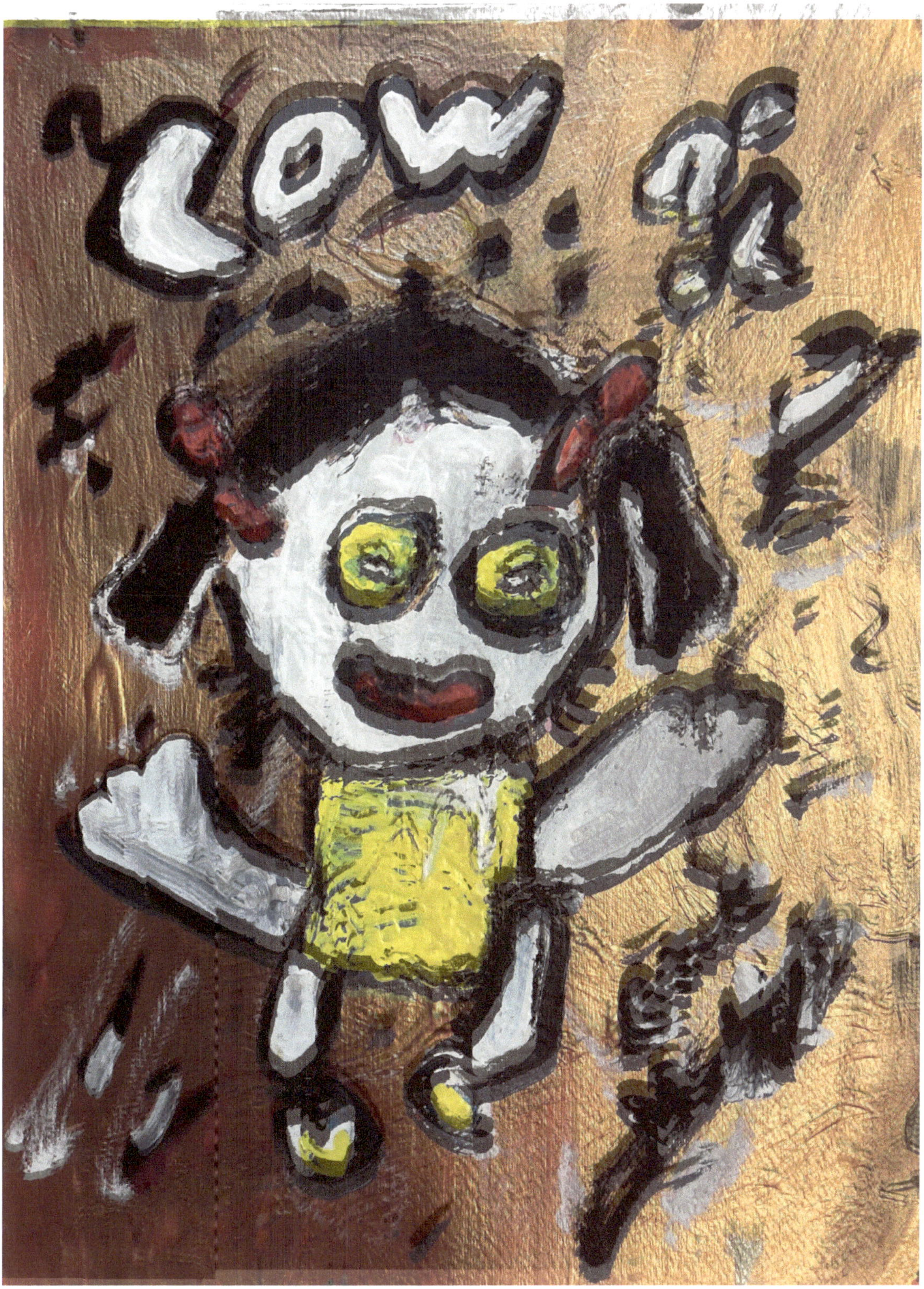
cow

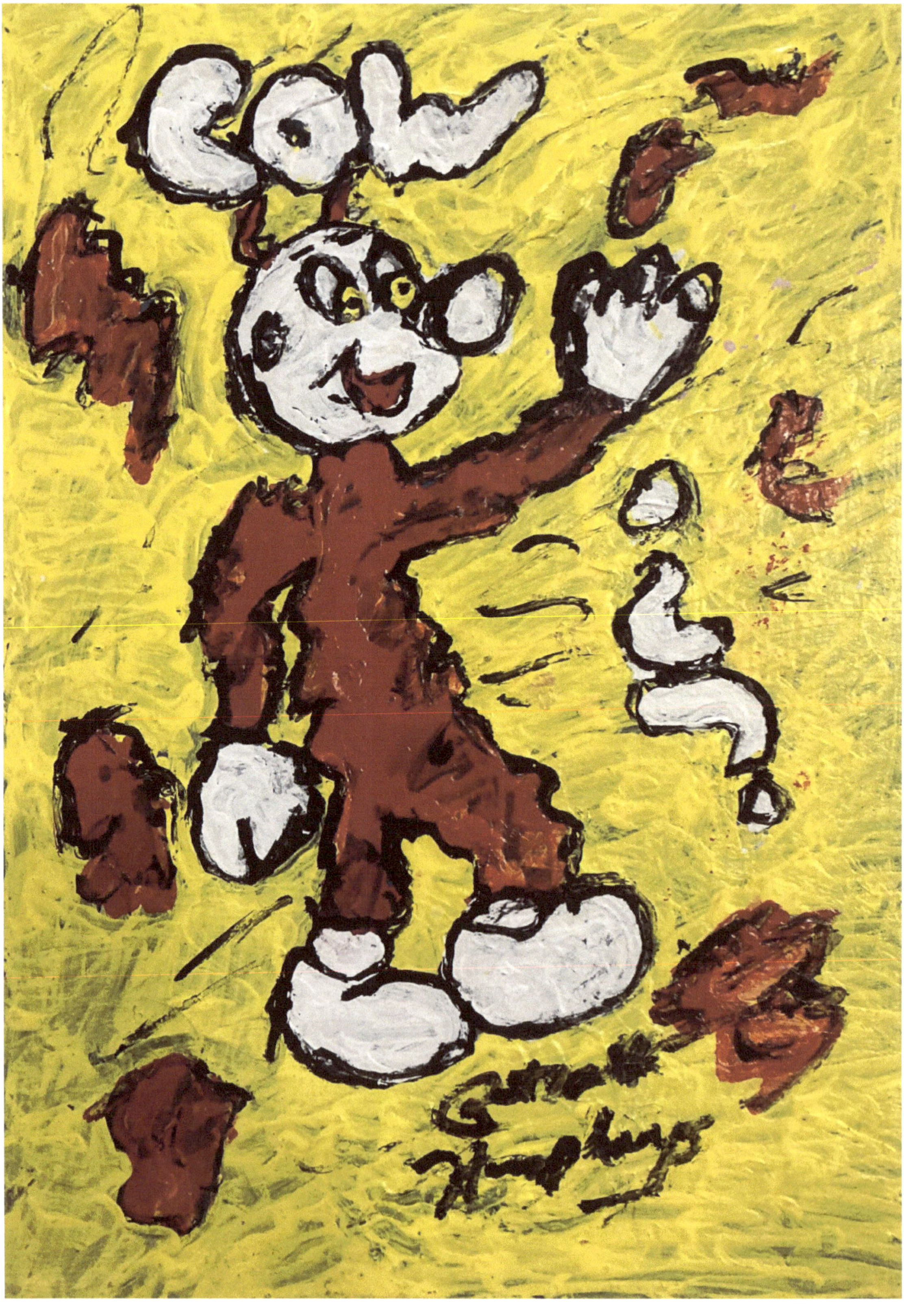
COW

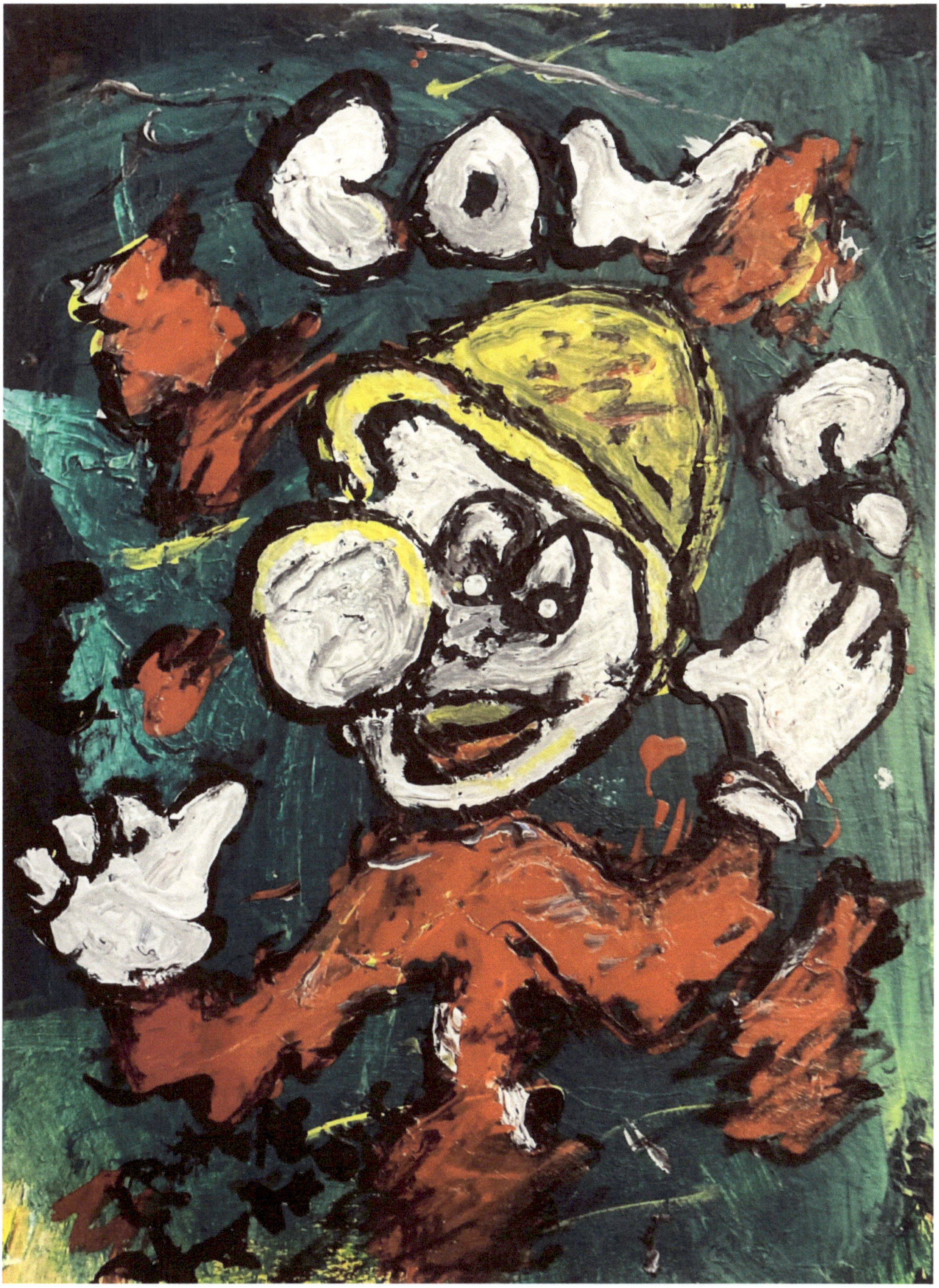

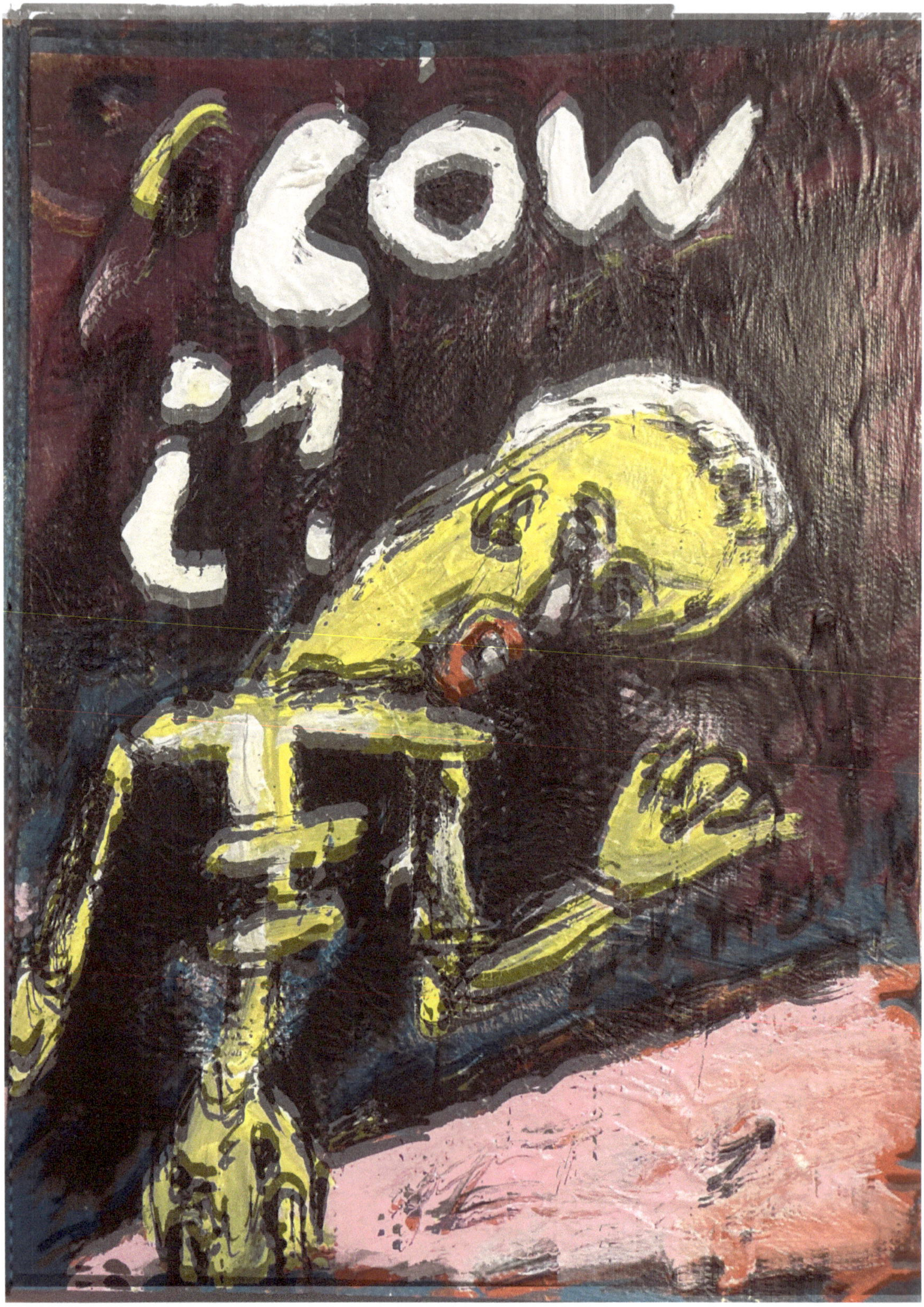
cow

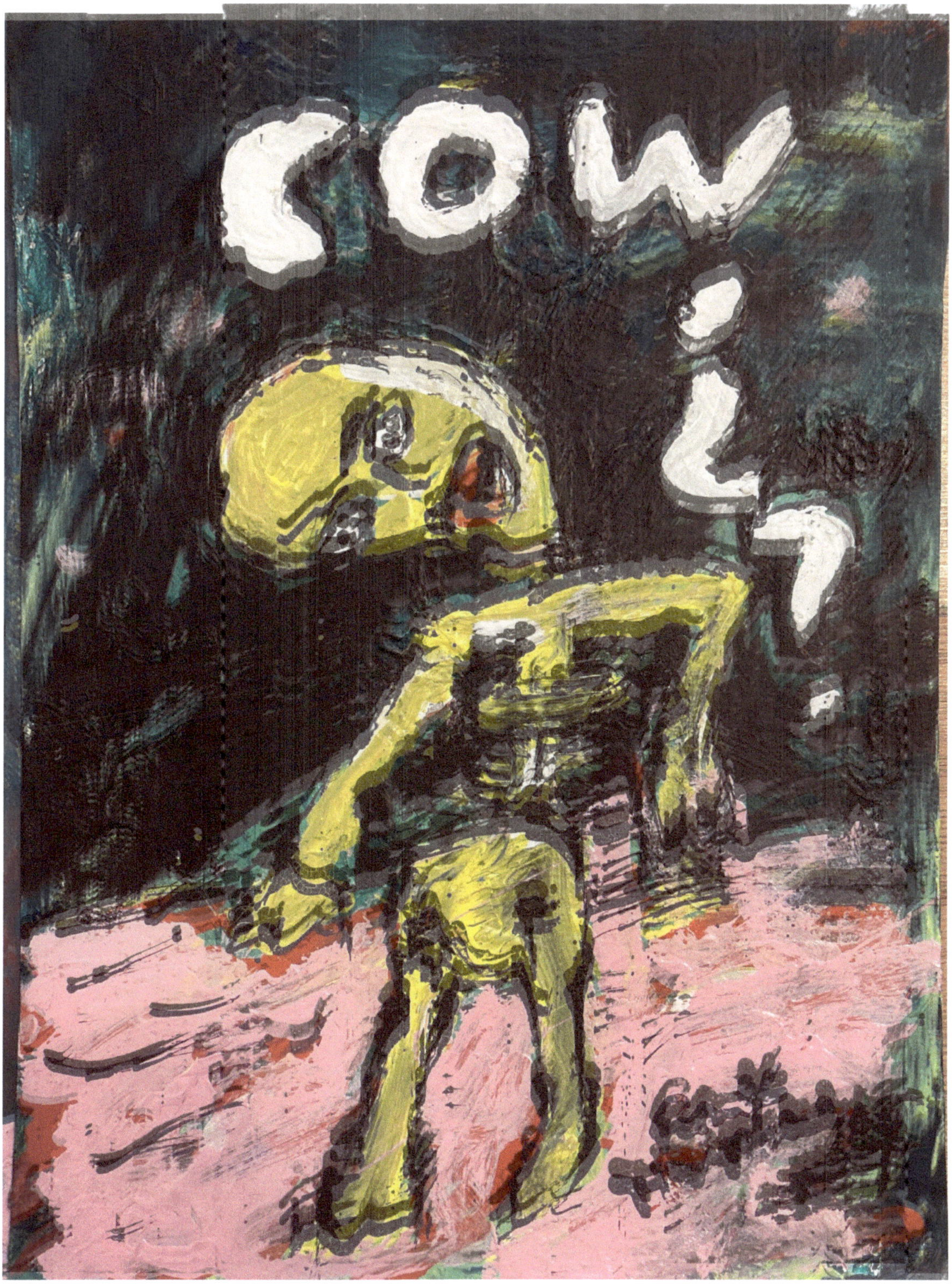
cow

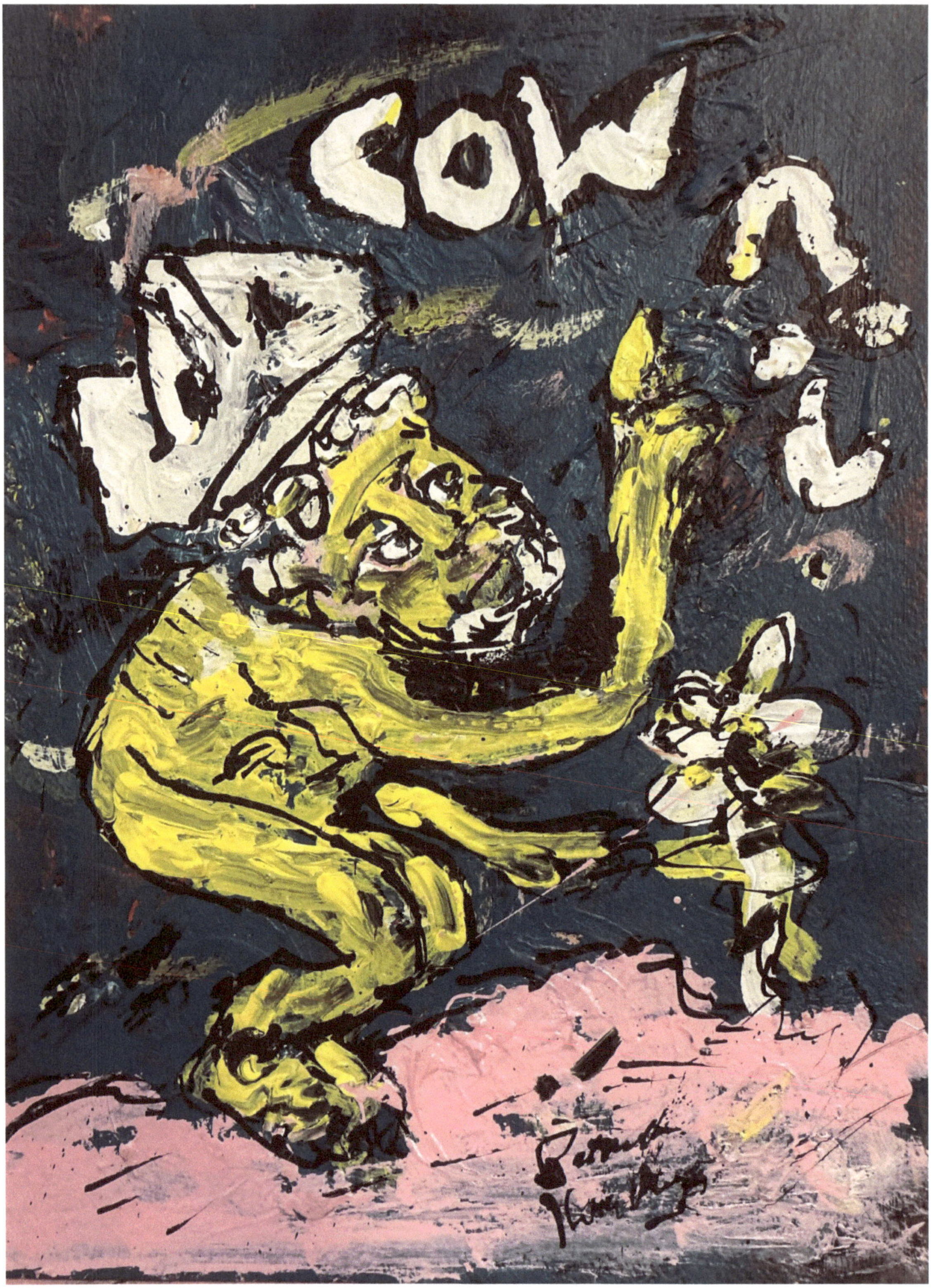
COW

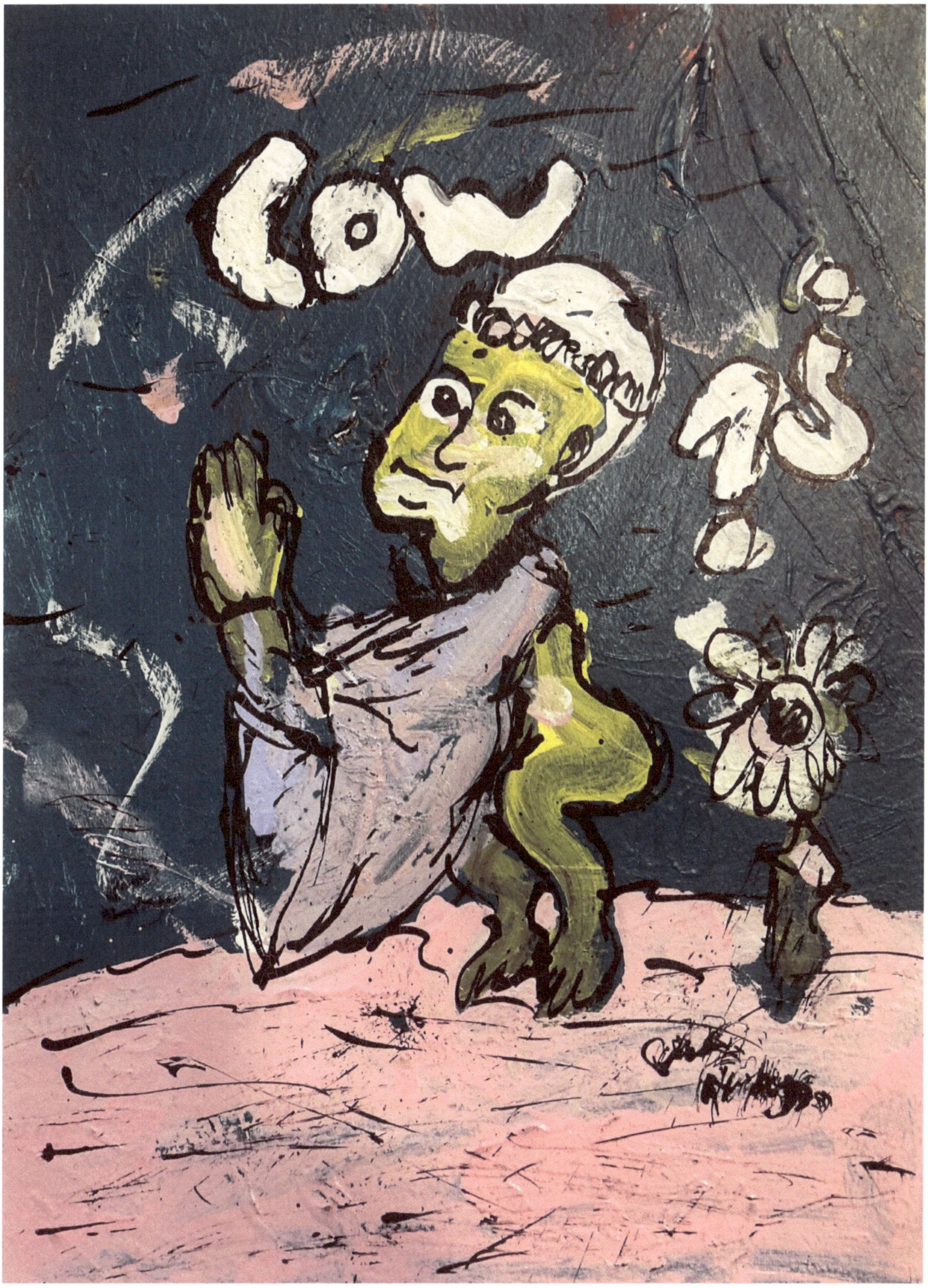
Cow ?!

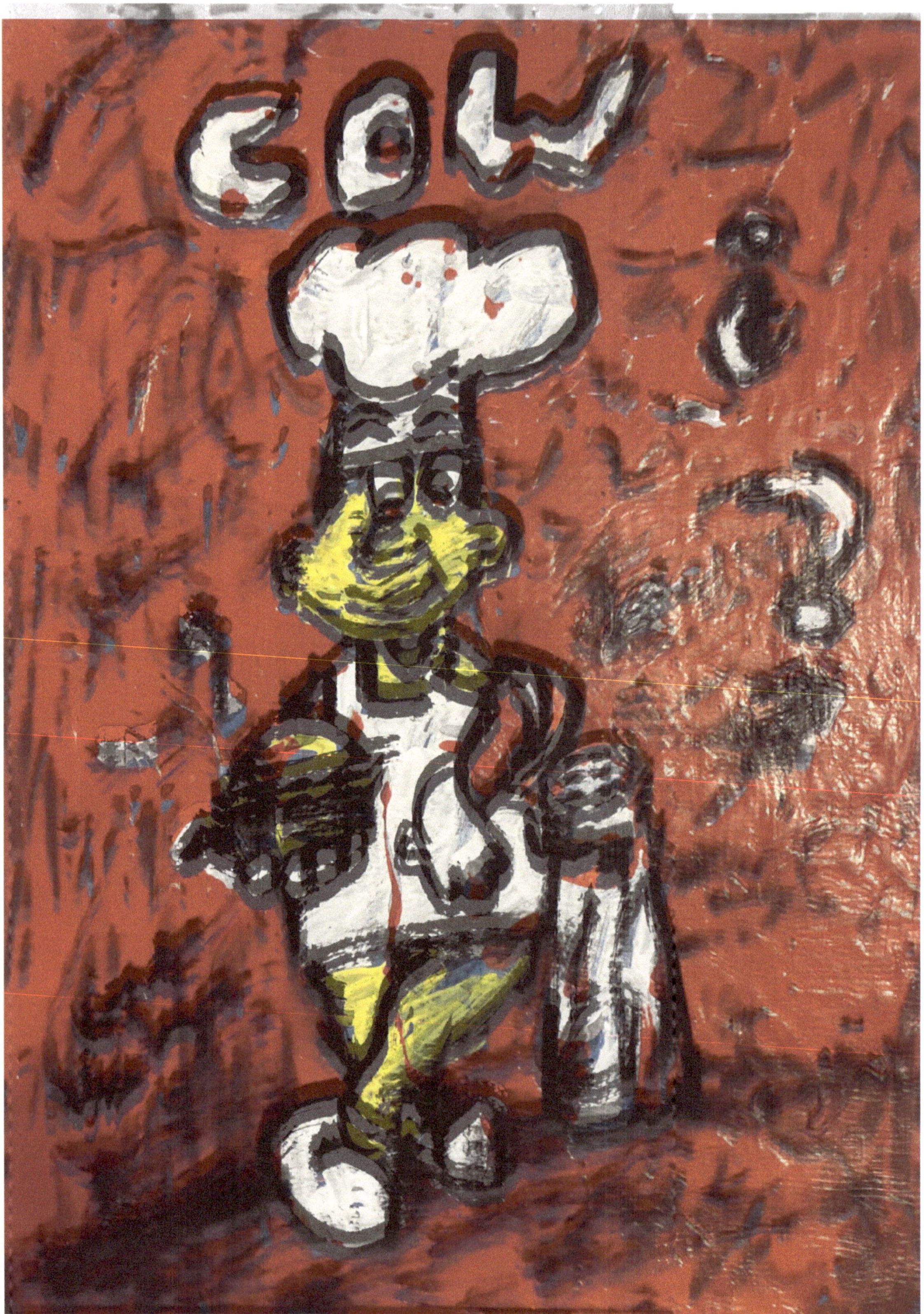
COW

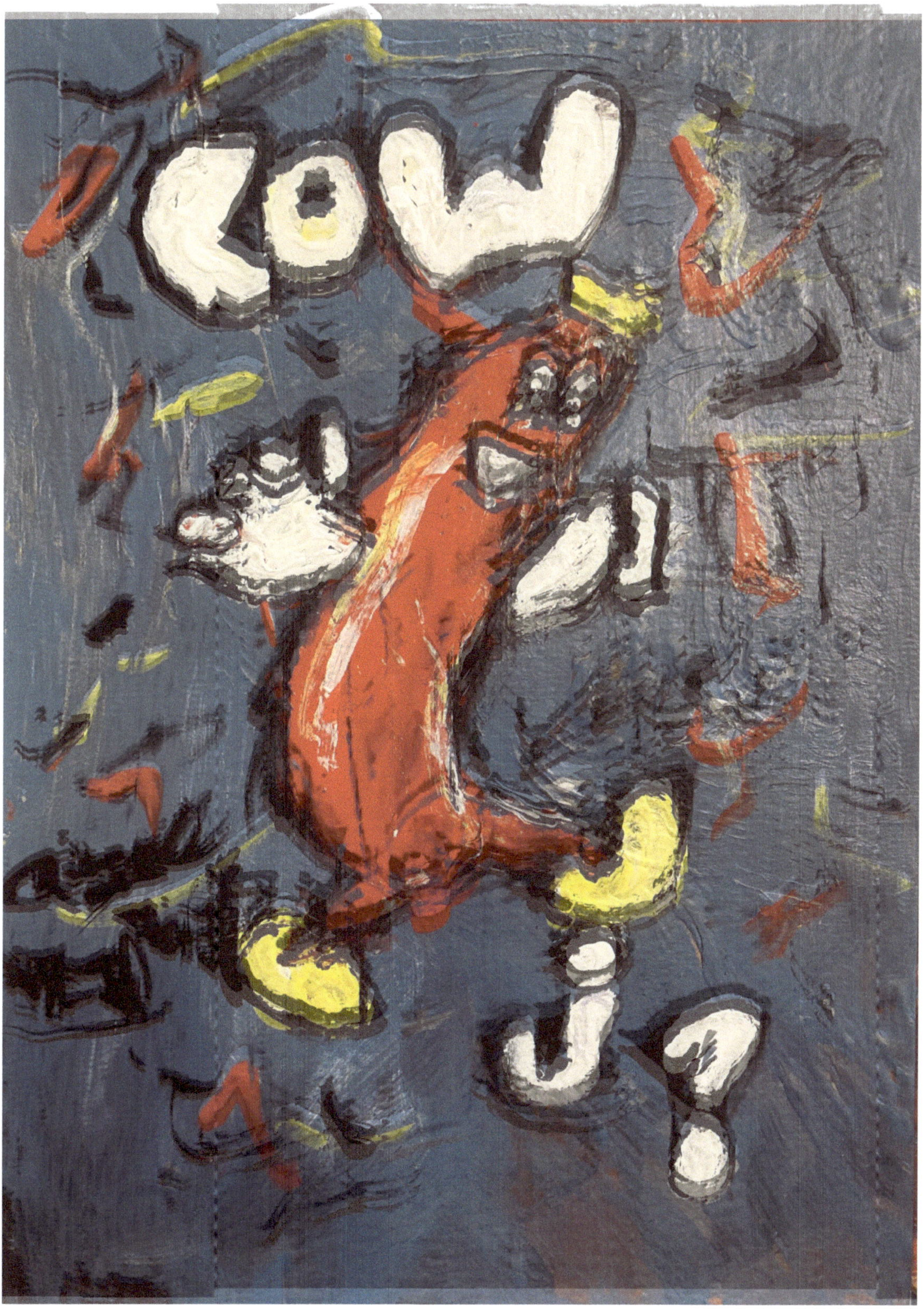
COW

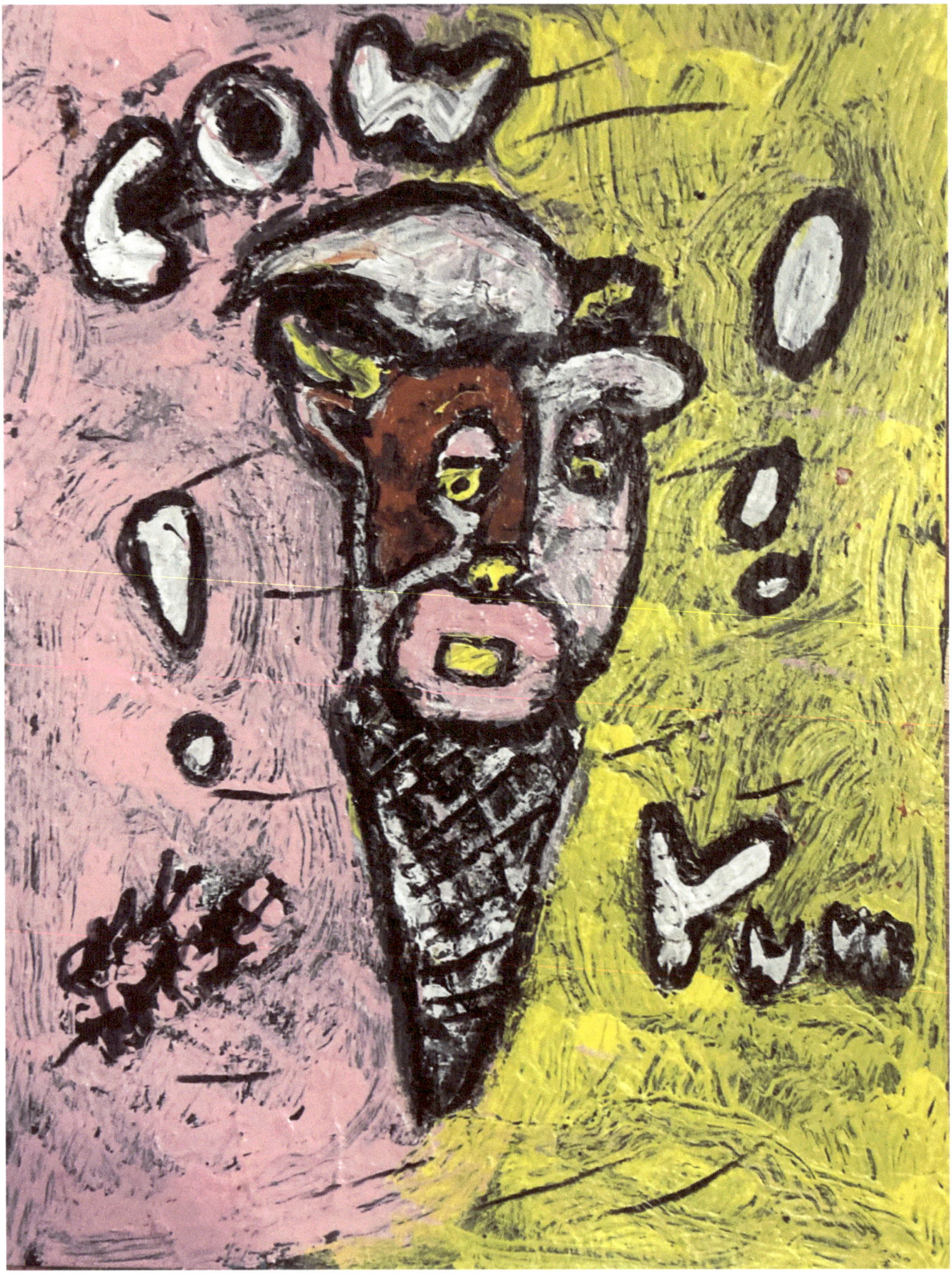
COW
Yum

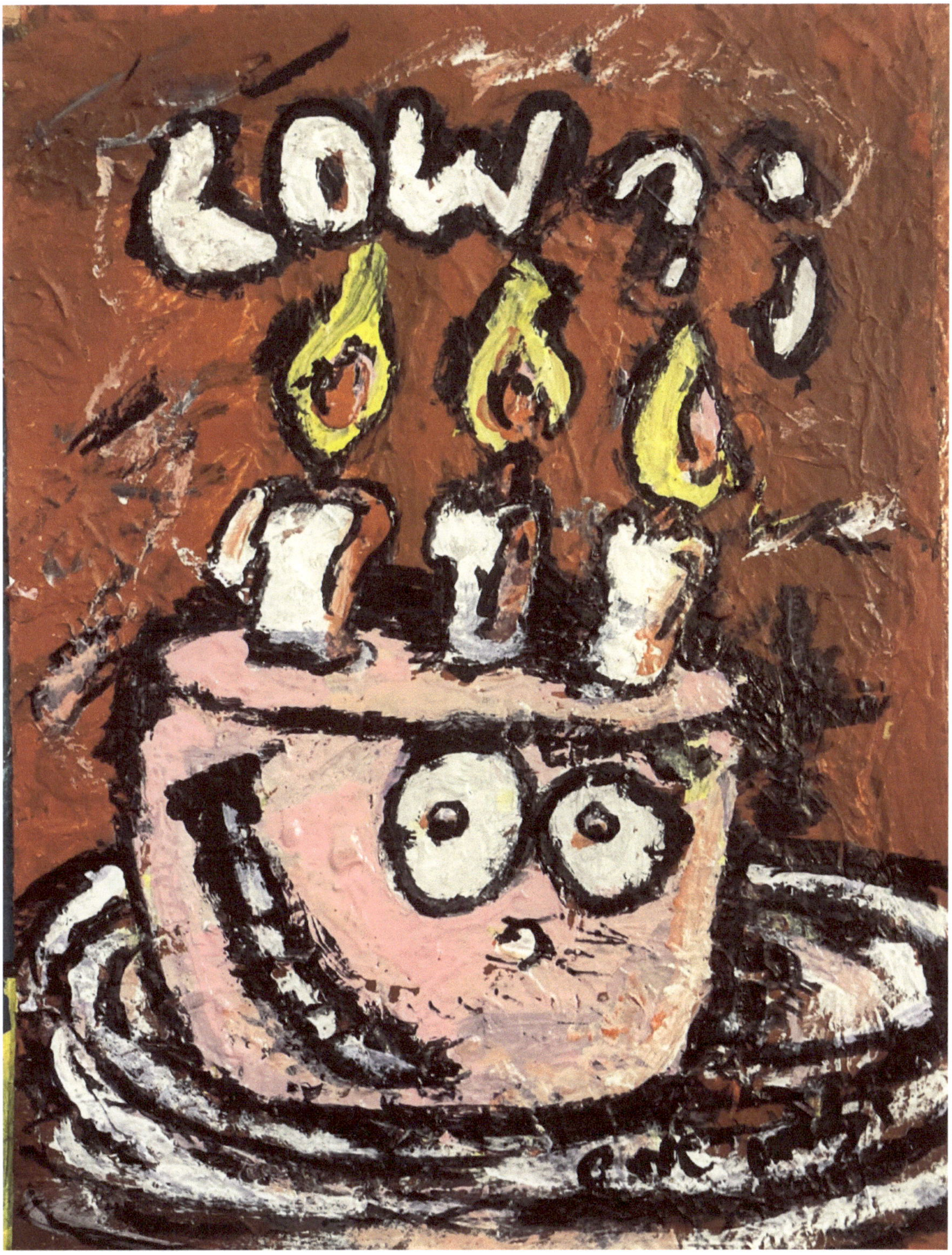

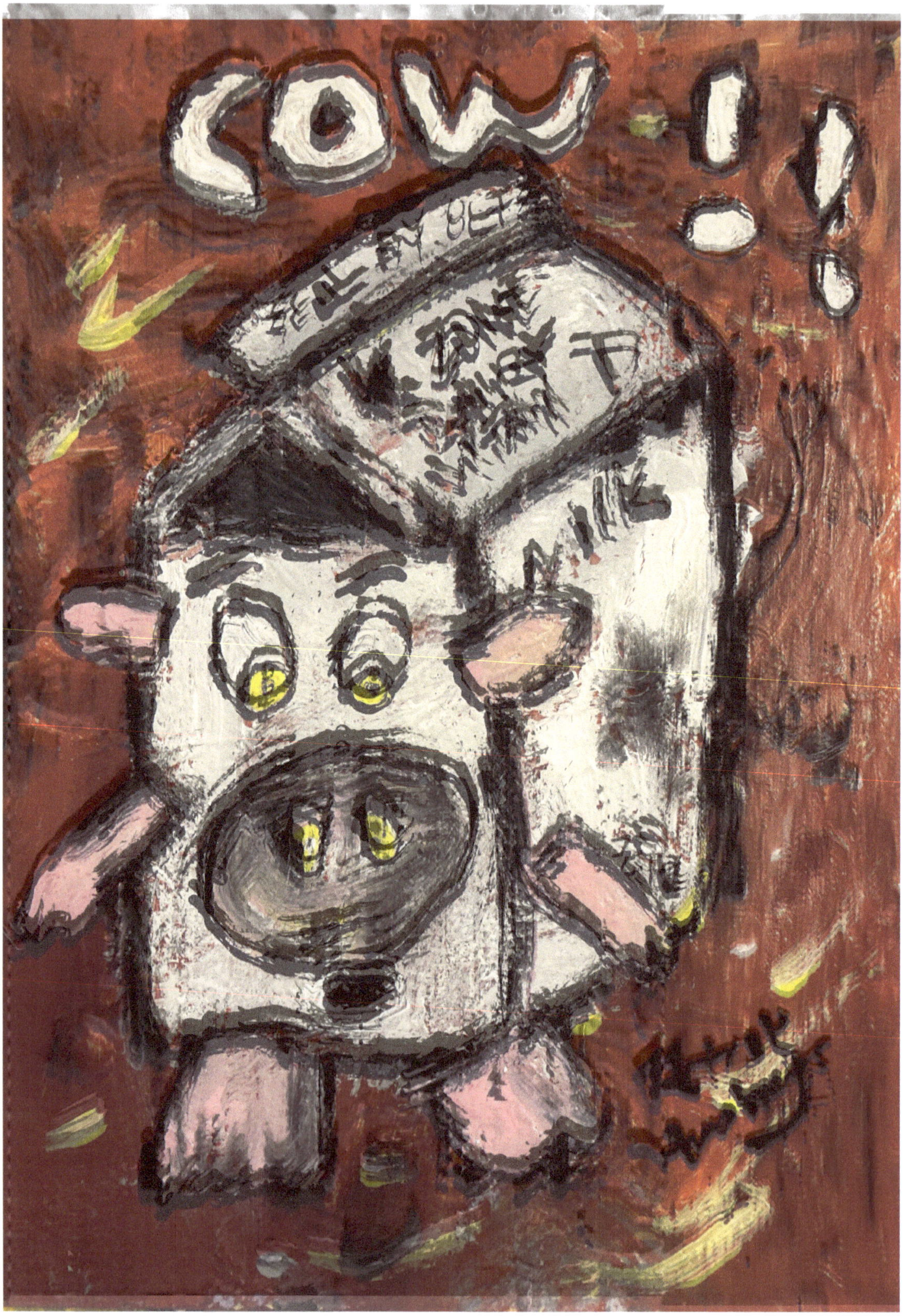
COW!!
MILK

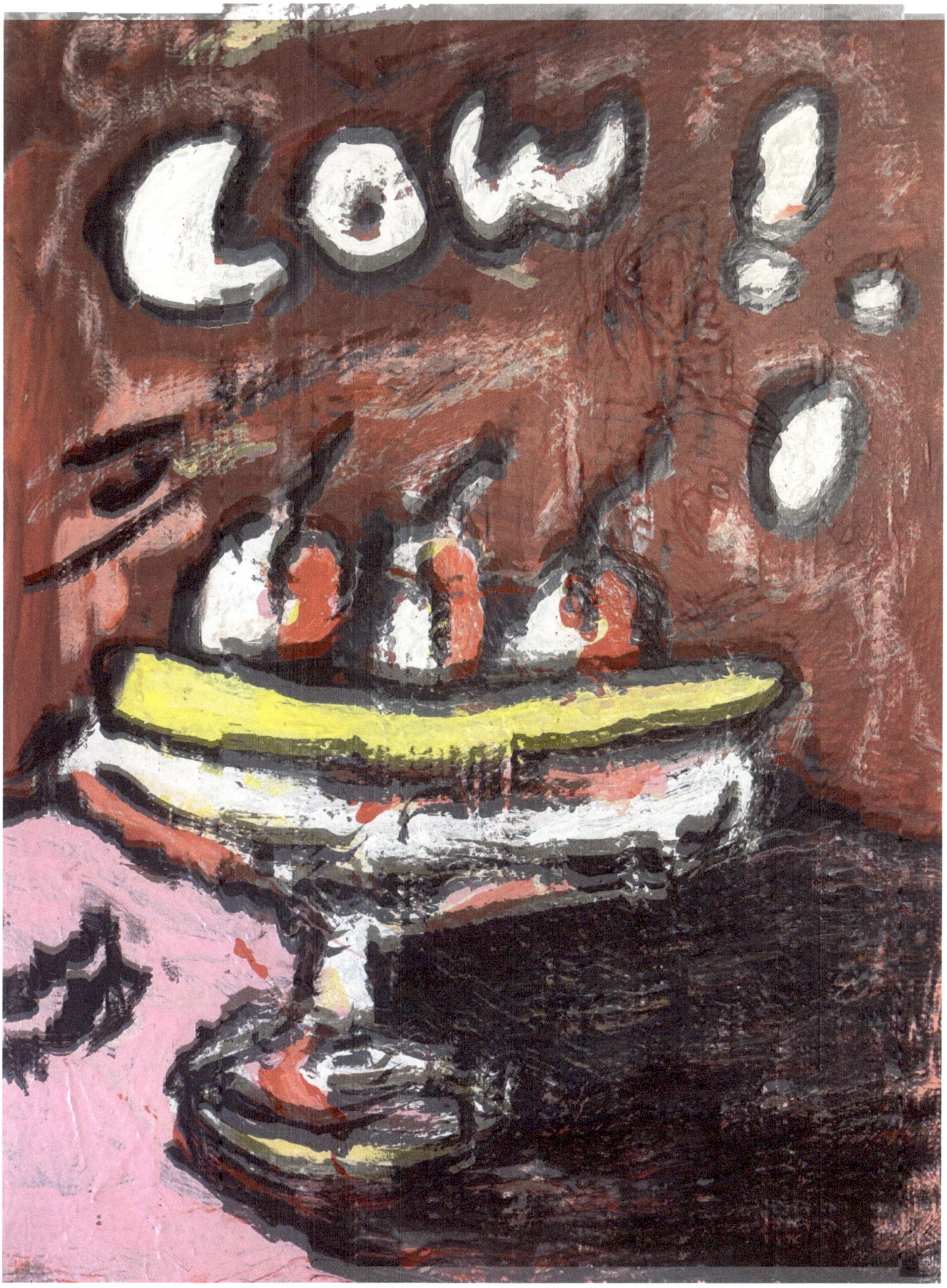
Cow!!

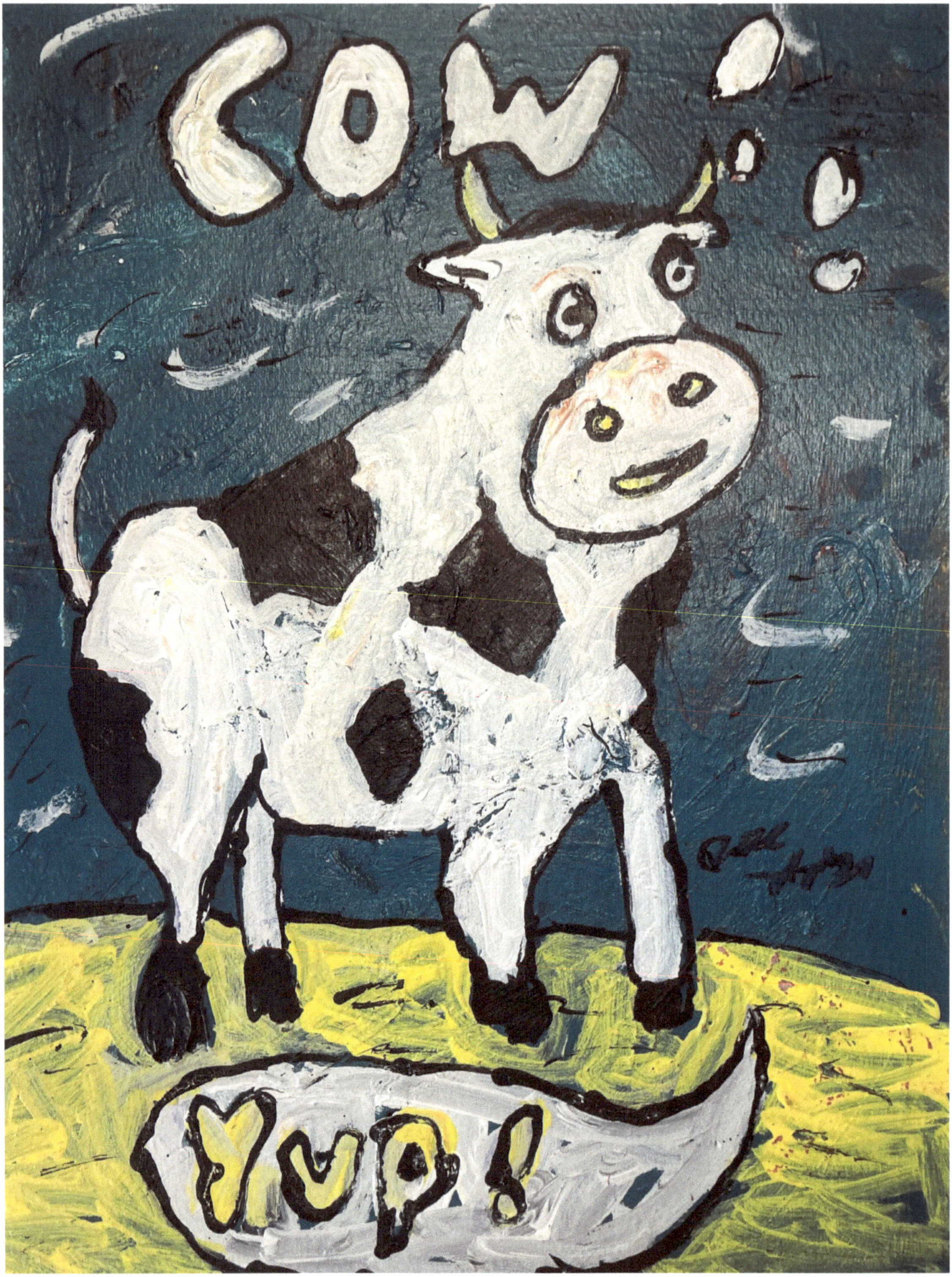
COW?
Yup!

www.ingramcontent.com/pod-product-compliance
Lightning Source LLC
Chambersburg PA
CBHW051944210526
45473CB00006B/2376